....

This book belongs to

....

Folded by

Color Editions No. 2

MICKEY MOUSE

featuring
The Wisdom of Walt Disney

Studio Fun Books
White Plains, New York • Montréal, Québec • Bath, United Kingdom

ArtFolds™
Color Editions No. 2
Mickey Mouse © 2014 Disney Enterprises, Inc.

ArtFolds is a patent-pending process for folding pages based on a set of unique printed marks to create a sculpture out of a bound book.

To learn more about ArtFolds, visit artfolds.com

Customized and/or prefolded ArtFolds are available. To explore options and pricing, email specialorder@artfolds.com.

To discover the wide range of products available from Studio Fun International, visit studiofun.com

Address any comments about ArtFolds to:
Publisher
Studio Fun Books
44 South Broadway, 7th floor
White Plains, NY 10601

Or send an email to publisher@artfolds.com.

Printed in China
Conforms to ASTM F963

1 3 5 7 9 10 8 6 4 2 LPP/04/14
ISBN 978-0-7944-3221-8

About ArtFolds

THE BOOK YOU HOLD in your hands is more than just a book. It's an ArtFolds! Inside are simple instructions that will show you how to fold the pages to transform this book into a beautiful Mickey Mouse-shaped sculpture. No special skill is required; all you'll do is carefully fold the corners of marked book pages, based on the folding lines provided. When complete, you'll have created a long-lasting work of art. It's fun and easy, and can be completed in just one evening!

To add to the experience, each ArtFolds contains compelling reading content. In this edition, you'll discover words of wisdom from Walt Disney, the creator of Mickey Mouse.

Each ArtFolds edition is designed by an established, professional book sculptor whose works are routinely displayed and sold in art galleries, museum shops, and online crafts and art stores. ArtFolds celebrates this community of artists and encourages you to support this expanding art form by seeking out their work and sharing their unique designs and creations with others.

To learn more about ArtFolds, visit **artfolds.com.** There you'll find details of all ArtFolds editions, instructional videos, and much more.

Instructions

Creating your ArtFolds Color Editions book sculpture is easy! Just follow these simple instructions and guidelines:

1. Always fold right-hand pages.

2. Always fold toward you.

3. All folding pages require two folds: The top corner will fold down, and the bottom corner will fold up.

4. Grasp the top right corner of the page, and fold until the side of the page aligns exactly with the TOP of the horizontal color bar.

5. Grasp the bottom right corner of the page, and fold upward until the side of the page aligns exactly with the BOTTOM of the horizontal color bar.

6. Carefully run your finger across the folds to make sure they are straight, crisp, and accurate.

7. Continue on to the next page and repeat until your ArtFolds book sculpture is complete!

Extra advice

- We recommend washing and then thoroughly drying your hands prior to folding.

- Some folders prefer using a tool to help make fold lines straight and sharp. Bone folders, metal rulers, popsicle sticks, or any other firm, straight tool will work.

- Some folders prefer to rotate their book sideways to make folding easier.

- Remember: The more accurate you are with each fold, the more accurate your completed book sculpture will be!

Folding begins as soon as you turn the page and continues for the next 119 right-hand pages.

For more folding instructions and videos, visit **artfolds.com**

About Walt Disney

Walt Disney is famous as the creator of Mickey Mouse, but Mickey was not his first animated star. Oswald the Lucky Rabbit, created by the Disney Bros.' Studio, Walt's first venture in Hollywood, was very popular, but Walt lost the rights to Oswald in 1928. (It was not until 2006 that the Walt Disney Company reacquired the rights to Oswald.) After that setback, Walt Disney was inspired to create Mickey Mouse, relating a story about a tame mouse who had lived in one of his studios. Even the most famous mouse in the world did not meet with instant success. Disney couldn't secure distribution for the first animated shorts to feature Mickey, but when Disney added sound to the mix—providing the voice and personality for Mickey Mouse himself, as he would do until 1947—Mickey Mouse become a hit.

During his life, Walt Disney was nominated for 59 Academy Awards® and won 26. His studio pioneered feature-length animated films and expanded into live-action feature films and television. Fulfilling a lifelong dream, he opened Disneyland park in California, which led to Florida's Walt Disney World. By the early 1960s, Walt Disney's company was the leading family entertainment producer.

Disney's own words, which you'll read here, reflect the way he lived his life. You'll see that he prized creativity, resourcefulness, and determination. And he had a special regard for the imagination of children, which inspired his own inventive vision.

"We keep moving forward—
opening up new doors and new
things—because we're curious.
And curiosity keeps leading us
down new paths."

"Every child is born blessed
with a vivid imagination.
But just as a muscle grows
flabby with disuse, so the
bright imagination of a child
pales in later years if he
ceases to exercise it."

"Somehow I can't believe that there are many heights that can't be scaled by a man who knows the secret of making dreams come true. The special secret, it seems to me, can be summarized in four Cs. They are Curiosity, Confidence, Courage, and Constancy, and the greatest of these is Confidence."

"People often ask me if I know the secret of success and if I could tell others how to make their dreams come true. My answer is, you do it by working."

"The way to get started is to quit
talking and begin doing."

"A lot of young people think the future is closed to them, that everything has been done. This is not so. There are still plenty of avenues to be explored. To the youngsters of today, I say believe in the future, the world is getting better; there is still plenty of opportunity."

"Get a good idea, and stay with
it. Dog it, and work at it until it's
done, and done right."

"It's kind of fun to do the impossible."

"I can never stand still. I must explore and experiment. I am never satisfied with my work. I resent the limitations of my own imagination."

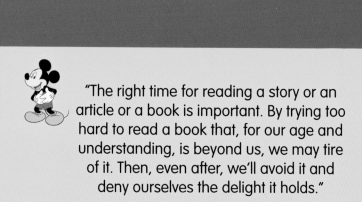

"The right time for reading a story or an article or a book is important. By trying too hard to read a book that, for our age and understanding, is beyond us, we may tire of it. Then, even after, we'll avoid it and deny ourselves the delight it holds."

"All the adversity I've had in my life, all my troubles and obstacles, have strengthened me."

"Don't stick too closely to your favorite subject. That would keep you from adventuring into other fields. It's silly to build a wall around your interests."

"In bad times and good, I have never lost my sense of zest for life."

"Why worry? If you've done the very best you can, worrying won't make it any better. I worry about many things, but not about water over the dam."

"In order to make good in your chosen task, it's important to have someone you want to do it for. The greatest moments in life are not concerned with selfish achievements but rather with the things we do for the people we love and esteem, and whose respect we need."

"Money—or, rather the lack of
it to carry out my ideas—may
worry me, but it does not excite
me. Ideas excite me."

"I think of a newborn baby's mind as a blank book. During the first years of his life much will be written on the pages. The quality of the writing, whatever it be, will affect his life profoundly."

"I have been up against
tough competition all my life.
I wouldn't know how to get
along without it."

"Essentially, the real difference
between a child and an adult
is experience."

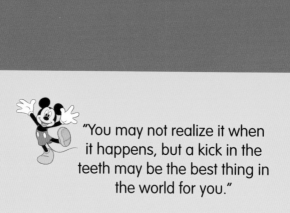

"You may not realize it when it happens, but a kick in the teeth may be the best thing in the world for you."

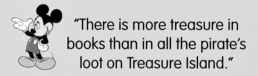

"There is more treasure in books than in all the pirate's loot on Treasure Island."

"Children are people, and they should have to reach to learn about things, to understand things, just as adults have to reach if they want to grow in mental stature."

"Leadership implies a strong faith
or belief in something."

"I always like to look on the optimistic side of life, but I am realistic enough to know that life is a complex matter."

"Courage is the main quality of
leadership, in my opinion, no
matter where it is exercised.
Usually it implies some risk—
especially in new undertakings.
Courage to initiate something
and to keep it going—pioneering
and adventurous spirit to blaze
new ways, often, in our land
of opportunity."

"Life is composed of lights and shadows,
and we would be untruthful, insincere,
and saccharine if we tried to pretend
there were no shadows."

"The way to keep children out of trouble is to keep them interested in things. Lecturing to children is no answer to delinquency. Preaching won't keep kids out of trouble. But keeping their minds occupied will."

"You'll be a poorer person all
your life if you don't know some
of the great stories and the
great poems."

"It's a mistake not to give people a chance to learn to depend on themselves while they are young."

"I suppose my formula might
be: dream, diversify, and
never miss an angle."

"You can dream, create, design, and build the most wonderful place in the world … but it requires people to make the dream a reality."

The ArtFolds Portfolio

Color Editions

These smaller ArtFolds™ editions use a range of colors printed on each page to make each sculpture a multi-colored work of art. Titles now or soon available include:

Edition 1: Heart
Edition 2: Mickey Mouse
Edition 3: Christmas Tree
Edition 4: MOM
Edition 5: Flower

Classic Editions

These larger ArtFolds™ editions include the full text of a classic book; when folded, book text appears along the edges, creating a piece of art that celebrates the dignity and beauty of a printed book. Titles now or soon available include:

Edition 1: LOVE
Edition 2: Snowflake
Edition 3: JOY
Edition 4: READ
Edition 5: Sun

To see the full range of ArtFolds editions, visit artfolds.com.

About the Designer

The sculpture design in this edition was created exclusively for ArtFolds by Luciana Frigerio. Based in Vermont, Luciana has been making photographs, objects, book sculptures, and artistic mischief for over 30 years. Her work has been exhibited in galleries and museums around the world. Luciana's artwork can be found at: lucianafrigerio.com, and her unique, customized book sculptures can be found in her shop on the online crafts market Etsy at: etsy.com/shop/LucianaFrigerio.